SHOEGASM

AN EXPLOSION OF CUTTING-EDGE DESIGN

SHOEGASM

AN EXPLOSION OF CUTTING-EDGE DESIGN

Clare Anthony

Race Point
PUBLISHING
www.racepointpub.com
New York, NY

Race Point
PUBLISHING

A division of Book Sales, Inc.
276 Fifth Avenue Suite 206
New York, New York 10001

This 2012 edition published by Race Point Publishing by arrangement with
The Book Shop, Ltd.

DESIGN Tim Palin Creative

ISBN-13: 978-1-937994-01-3

Printed in China

2 4 6 8 10 9 7 5 3 1

www.racepointpub.com

CONTENTS

PREFACE

Architectural shoes are not new to me. By nature I adore theatrical and architectural shoes, especially the ones of Chau Har Lee. I saw her shoes for the first time when I was giving an award at the Royal College of Art, and I loved them. Straight away I recognized that she was a very promising designer.

This book illustrates shoes that are easy to design, but very difficult to execute and even harder to walk in. I am very glad that someone has come up with the wonderful idea of showing this force in design and the finished product that has resulted, which is fascinating in more ways than one.

I have been told numerous times by different young designers that I was responsible for the resurge of the extravagant silhouette of shoes. I am very happy and flattered to hear it. But I am even happier to see the range of marvelous ideas that are featured in this book, as without dreams and fantasy we are nothing.

This book will be a wonderful future testimony to how shoe design has progressed in time.

Manolo Blahnik

INTRODUCTION

Extreme shoes may seem to be a relatively recent phenomenon, but they've actually been around in one form or another for a very long time. Consider the solid gold sandals entombed with the pharaohs of ancient Egypt. Or the various kinds of platform shoes worn hundreds of years ago in China, Japan, the Ottoman Empire (bottom right), and Europe. In fifteenth-century Italy, platform shoes called chopines (bottom left) went as high as twenty inches. At the opposite extreme were the tiny shoes (top right) worn by Chinese women who underwent the painful process of foot-binding to achieve the ideal three-inch (or less) length of the golden lotus, as the bound foot was called.

In the sixteenth century, the high heel migrated to the West from the Middle East, where it was worn by horseback riders to help hold their feet in the stirrups. Although initially adopted by men, the heel was soon worn by upper-class members of both sexes.

To keep their heels from sinking into the muck of unpaved roads, men began wearing flat-soled mules that they could slip over their high-heeled shoes (right). The combination was called "slap sole," after the sound the sole made when it slapped against the heel as the wearer walked. By the early seventeenth century, slap soles had become the exclusive province of women, who wore them as indoor shoes. Today's skate shoes owe a debt to these early designs.

Louis XIV, the Sun King, upped the ante for status shoes when he declared that only members of the royal court could wear shoes with red heels. On men's shoes, high heels were blocky, but on women's, they were tapered.

After the French Revolution, high heels went out of style, but by the middle of the nineteenth century, they were back—at least for women. The first famous shoemaker was Jean-Louis François Pinet, whose beautifully embroidered shoes were sought after by wealthy, well-dressed women.

In the early twentieth century, Pietro Yantorny became the shoemaker of choice for the very rich. Outside his Paris shop, the sign read *Le bottier le plus cher du monde*—or, "The most expensive shoemaker in the world." His craftsmanship was exquisite, and it often took him up to two years to finish just one pair of shoes. A pair of mules (bottom left) from the late 1910s was modeled after Turkish harem slippers and embroidered with gold metallic thread.

André Perugia came to prominence in the 1920s, creating his own footwear designs and collaborating with couturiers such as Paul Poiret. In the 1930s, he partnered with Elsa Schiaparelli, a couturier who often incorporated surrealism in her clothes. In 1938, Schiaparelli and Perugia collaborated on a pair of high heel boots decorated with long monkey fur. Perugia was also the creator of the first towering heel-less shoe, which appeared in the late 1930s.

Around the same time, Salvatore Ferragamo introduced modern cork platforms and the wedge heel. One of his designs with a high platform in the colors of the rainbow (bottom right) is said to be a style he originally created for Judy Garland. His designs were sought after by both male and female actors, earning him the sobriquet of "Shoemaker to the Stars."

Throughout his sixty-year career, Roger Vivier experimented with heel shapes (below) and extravagant embellishments, including beads, pearls, rhinestones, feathers, and intricate embroidery. In the early 1950s, he was one of the first, if not *the* first, to use World War II technology to create needle-thin stiletto heels. In 1953, Vivier went to work for Christian Dior, where he made fashion history as the first shoe designer to share a label with a couturier.

Beth Levine started out as a shoe model and ended up as head designer at I. Magnin. In 1948, she opened a shoe company with her husband, Herbert Levine. Although the company bore his name, Beth Levine was the creative genius behind the label. Among her creations were stocking shoes (right), topless shoes that adhered to the foot with adhesive, spring-o-lator sandals, shoes with rolled-leather heels, and "Kabuki" shoes, which were inspired by Asian footwear. Levine also experimented with unusual materials, such as paper and Astroturf.

In the 1960s, flats were once again in style. Courrège's space-age-style and go-go boots exemplified the Mod look, and Charles Jourdan created playful Op-Art accessories. Birkenstock sandals became the symbol of the "back to nature" look. But high heels did not go away and, by the early 1970s, they were once again being worn—by both men and women.

Platform shoes came back in a big way in the 1970s. They were worn everywhere, from the street to the stage. Male rock groups seemed to compete for the title of most outrageous costume, including platform shoes, with KISS (below) among the top contenders.

In the 1980s, humor made an appearance in the footwear of several designers. A pair of pumps from Susan Bennis/Warren Edwards featured leather appliqués of brightly colored splotches containing the words *pop*, *pow*, and *power*. Tokio Kumagaï hand-painted his shoes in designs inspired by artists such as Salvador Dali and Wassily Kandinsky. He also produced whimsical pumps with the faces of animals on the toes. Isabel Canovas created hot-pink heels with ants made of black sequins crawling up the sides and a flat that looked like a partially peeled banana.

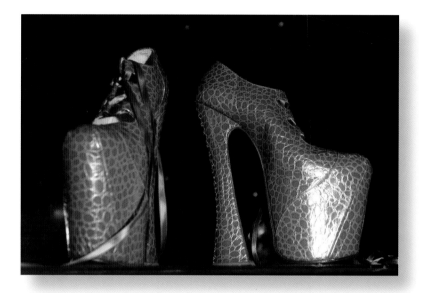

In the 1990s, Vivienne Westwood revived platform shoes, taking them to even more towering heights (top right). In 1993, model Naomi Campbell took a spill while walking the runway in a pair of eight-inch-high Westwood platforms. Since then, the style has never really gone out of style. In fact, platforms just continue to get higher and higher.

Although extreme shoes have existed for hundreds of years, there were rarely so many different kinds co-existing at the same time as there are today. In *Shoegasm*, you'll find towering platforms and sexy stilettos, pumps made with fabric that emits light, slotted shoes that can be taken apart and packed flat, shoes that are formed out of liquid in a rotational mold, and even shoes that are printed out in 3D. And then there are simply delightful designs, like those of Mihai Albu (bottom left) and Naäm Ben (bottom right), whose playful exuberance is guaranteed to make you smile.

ALAIN QUILICI
Extending and Redefining

Japanese films, cyborgs, artificial environments, the work of painters Egon Schiele and Francis Bacon—all provide creative inspiration for Alain Quilici. Quilici worked in the family shoe business in Tuscany before studying fashion design at the Polimoda Fashion Institute in Florence and at the London College of Fashion. He launched his first women's footwear collection in 2007, overseeing the production process from start to finish.

Quilici thinks of shoes as extending and redefining the body. Although he restricts his palette to black, white, and neutral colors, he allows his imagination to roam freely, drawing ideas from dreams and reality, nature and technology, transformation and evolution. The vertically slashed wedge is one of his signature styles, appearing on sandals (opposite page), boots, and clogs.

"Taking from my mind all that I've seen, looking for what has never been . . ."

—Anastasia Radevich

The source of Radevich's inspiration for the Kinetik collection was a visit to the Montreal Electro-Industrial Noize Festival of the same name. Despite the delicate look of the intricate sculptural heels, the shoes are functional as well as aesthetically stunning. Two styles have patches of fiber optic material that make them glow with an otherworldly light.

"I want to bring a fresh perspective to fashion, fusing the mastery and traditions of making with a visionary approach."

—Andreia Chaves

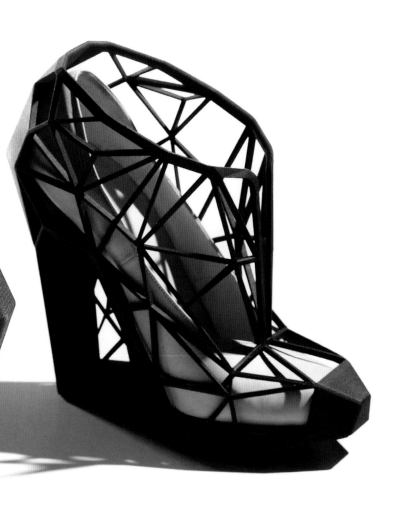

Continuing the theme of camouflage, Chaves created "Naked." For this shoe, she tucked a neutral-colored leather pump that blends with the foot inside a geometric black cage made of 3D-printed nylon.

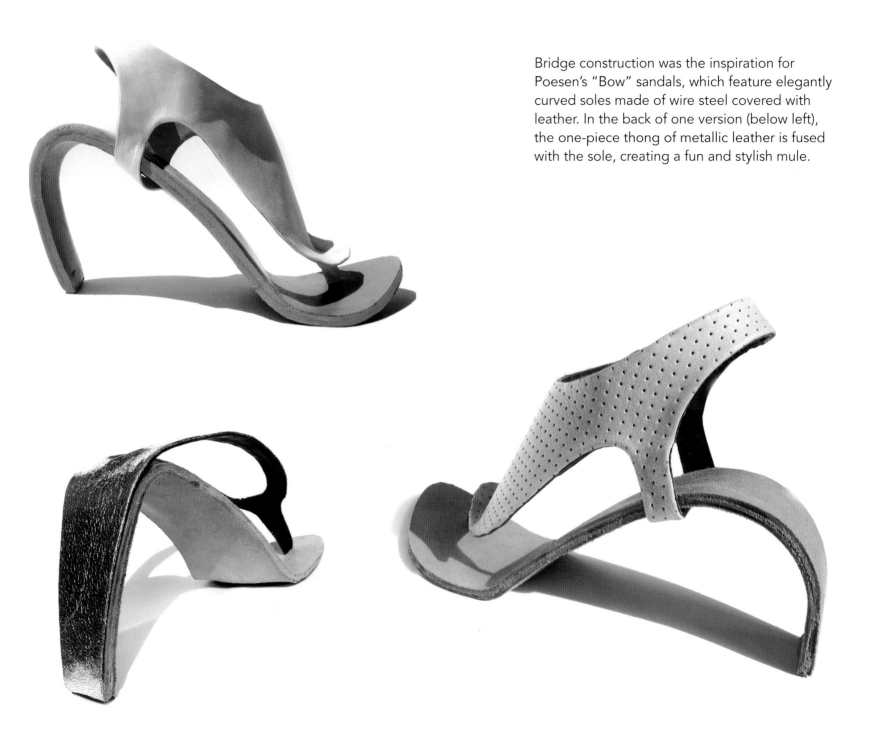

Bridge construction was the inspiration for Poesen's "Bow" sandals, which feature elegantly curved soles made of wire steel covered with leather. In the back of one version (below left), the one-piece thong of metallic leather is fused with the sole, creating a fun and stylish mule.

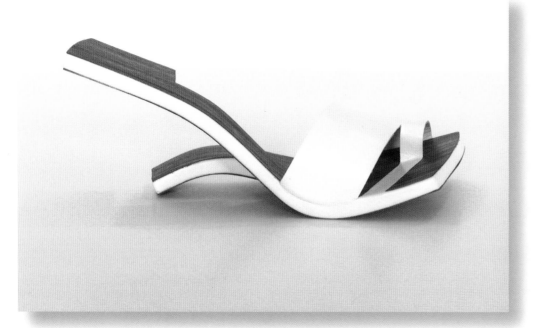

"Cuoio" (below) was inspired by vegetable-tanned bottom leather, which is strong and rigid. To form the wedge heel, Poesen folded a wide strip of undried leather back and forth in two columns with a loop between them. The bottom sole gracefully curves up and around at front and back to form the insole, and a tapering strip of leather winds across the ankle, through the wedge, and back over the instep and toe.

Poesen made the sole of "Trix" (above) from carbon fiber covered with a layer of rosewood, which she cut and bent to form the arch and the heel. For the strap, she used a single piece of leather cut to form a wide band over the instep and a narrow strip for the toe loop.

"I love the challenge of looking at traditional footwear methods in a new way. It takes you out of your comfort zone."

—Chau Har Lee

At Cordwainers, Chau Har Lee learned traditional shoemaking, but at the Royal College, she was exposed to people working in other design areas—architects, engineers, product designers—and realized that to make a shoe she "didn't need twenty different components—leather, tacks, and glue. It's about stripping everything down to the basics." Looking at the framework of a shoe and analyzing its construction led her to create flat pieces that could be slotted together to form an attractive shoe, such as the one shown here. The key was designing a structure that had strength in the right places to support the foot.

Louboutin collaborated with Jean-François Lesage, master embroiderer, to create "Marie Antoinette," an extravagant shoe made even more precious by the fact that only thirty-six of each color—blue, yellow, and pink—were produced. In eighteenth-century France, Marie Antoinette and the women of her court wore elaborate, themed hairstyles up to three feet high. On the ankle strap of Louboutin's shoe, intricate embroidery depicts the queen in one of her most famous hairstyles, which celebrated France's alignment with America in the Revolutionary War. At the top, among waves of hair, perches a French frigate that had won a key battle with the British.

Only a superheroine with a weakness for Christian Louboutin shoes would dare to wear "Kryptonite," with its bristling spikes at heel and toe. Crystals of varying sizes dot the tulle upper, gathering most thickly beneath the spikes at the heel and trailing down the metallic textured calfskin of the stiletto.

Although she thinks it's necessary to be aware of trends, Lundsten tends not to follow them, preferring to "create something new and unique." For her shoes, which are handmade in Brazil, she chooses sustainable wood and leathers that are byproducts of other industries. However, she uses these traditional materials in new ways, experimenting with shape, color, and detail. This willingness to experiment—which she believes is "the best way to push design forward"—is clearly evident in her Project 2 (opposite page) and Project 3 (right) creations.

54

FINSK designs have been featured in major fashion magazines, including *Vogue*, *Elle*, and *Harper's Bazaar*. Lundsten won the Manolo Blahnik Award two years in a row while still a graduate student, and in *W* magazine, Blahnik was quoted as saying he was captivated by her work, adding, "It is like nothing anybody is doing at the moment, exquisite, divine, perfect."

Lundsten also creates runway footwear for fashion designers. When Basso & Brooke were planning their "Neo-Pop" themed spring/summer 2010 collection, they were looking for shoes that would not only reflect their vision but also stand out in their own right. They went to FINSK, and Lundsten designed shoes that combined the bright colors of the clothing with her trademark sculptural details (page 51 and opposite page). That same season, models for Ports 1961 also wore Lundsten's designs on the catwalk (left).

FRANCESCA CASTAGNACCI
TREADING LIGHTLY

Italian accessory designer Francesca Castagnacci combines traditional
craftsmanship with modern technology to create high-tech shoes that not
only are beautiful but also glow with light. Wanting to create accessories that
were more than passive objects, Castagnacci researched the possibility of
using fiber optics, long hair-like strands of glass, and LEDs to create shoes
and other accessories that take on a life of their own. She settled on Luminex,
a light-emitting fabric by an Italian manufacturer of the same name.

To create her asymmetrical half sandal/half bootie (opposite page),
Castagnacci elegantly folded and pleated the gray Luminex fabric, which is
left visible on the top and inside of the foot. She then ran leather and kidskin
up from the outside sole to end in Möbius-like loops over the top
of the shoe. The stiletto heel is silver plated.

"I wanted my accessories to shine like galaxies."

—Francesca Castagnacci

Castagnacci did not start out as a shoe designer but as a jewelry designer, with a degree from the Faculty of Architecture at the University of Florence. While working in Ireland, she entered a competition sponsored by Ferragamo that challenged designers to create shoes inspired by contemporary art—and won a scholarship for a graduate course in footwear and accessories at the Polimoda International Institute of Fashion Design & Marketing in Florence. In 2010, she took first prize in the first A & P Young competition for her light-emitting shoe designs.

Taminiau notes that Irradiance, his spring/summer 2011 collection, was based on the inner glow created by the "vulnerable yet positive" feeling you might have just before making a public appearance, when you "want to go onstage, but you're afraid and want to hide." The models wore masks, in keeping with the sense of wanting to hide, while the fluorescent yarn used in some of the materials gave an unmistakable glow to the designs. To accompany the clothes, Taminiau created spectacular modern versions of the chopines worn in Venice more than 500 years ago. The design shown here was worn by Beyoncé on the cover of her album, *Beyoncé 4*.

That same season, Taminiau introduced his first demi couture collection, entitled Separates, with more wearable, less expensive clothes than his haute couture designs. He described the collection as "feminine, sexy, and tough" with clothes in soft gold, beige, off-white, green, and pink. One of the shoes was definitely in keeping with the title of the show, looking like two designs—one in classic white satin and one covered with glamorous champagne-colored sequins—combined into one.

Tarnished Beauty, Taminiau's haute couture spring/summer 2012 collection, paired fragile fabrics in pastel colors with slightly tarnished over- and undergarments encrusted with glittering paillettes that simulated armor, and helmet-like headdresses. In the company press release, Taminiau said, "Beauty is more than a twinkling armor that protects us from reality. It is a hedonistic refuge that keeps the world outside. Real beauty comes alive when people open themselves to each other." The release also stated that the show was designed to elevate women. That was literally true of the shoes, although height has clearly been key to the footwear in most of Taminiau's collections.

It was also true in Poetic Clash, his fall/winter 2012–13 haute couture collection presented during Paris Fashion Week. Inspired by African patterns and the ikat fabrics of Uzbekistan, Taminiau added bold colors to his usually neutral palette, earning kudos from the critics. The shoe styles, as in his earlier shows, were lofty. From the side, the platform on each shoe slants inward from the toe, but about halfway to the floor, it juts back out in a near mirror image of the top half. In the back of each shoe, regardless of color or embellishment, a slim silver support runs from heel to floor.

JULIAN HAKES

a bridge for the foot

Julian Hakes is an architect with a specialty in bridge design. So perhaps it's not surprising that, sitting alone in his studio late one night, he started thinking about how he'd design a bridge for the foot. He considered which parts of the foot would bear the weight of the body. Then he wrapped tracing paper around his own foot, secured it with tape, and started drawing.

The design Hakes came up with began below the ball of the foot, wrapped around the instep, swept down to form the heel, and twisted back up to support the back of the foot and the ankle. An organic, sculptural design—and a radical one, given that there was no shank, or plate, to support the arch. But as Hakes says, the shoe is "not artificially supporting your foot where it doesn't need support."

With a carbon fiber core to give it spring, lots of padding to cushion the foot, and no shank, the "Mojito" makes the woman wearing it look and feel as if she's walking on air, Hakes says. When asked how the shoe got its name, he said that the design was fresh and light—a bit like a twist of lime in the Mojitos he'd had the night he'd designed it.

KOBI LEVI

a passion for shoes

Israeli shoe designer Kobi Levi creates wearable sculptures, crafting his shoes by hand from start to finish. Always fascinated with the shapes he saw in footwear, he made his first "shoe piece" in a tenth-grade art class, when he was asked to "draw a sculpture" with a metal wire. Levi created the shape of a high-heeled shoe that opened so you could put it on your foot.

He decided to concentrate on his passion for shoes in college at the Bezalel Academy of Arts and Design in Jerusalem, and specialized in footwear design and development. Now a freelance designer, Levi collaborates with companies in Italy, China, and Brazil as well as in Israel. He says each new design takes him about a month from sketch to prototype.

In a diner, the server asks if you want coffee and pours it into your cup. However, in the diner version of Levi's "Coffee" shoes, you can see the level of coffee in the pot going down as the coffee is poured, but what happened to the cup? Could the server have gotten distracted by someone walking by in another great pair of Kobi Levi shoes?

Can fire dragons, chopsticks, and slingshots be sexy? The answer is yes when it comes to Kobi Levi's footwear designs. For "Contemporary Chinese," he combined images of a fire dragon and chopsticks to create a sophisticated pair of stiletto heels.

Anyone who follows pop music will know that "Blond Ambition" was inspired by one of the costumes worn by Madonna for her 1990 world tour. The conical toes and side stitching come straight from the corset, and the heel perfectly mimics her hairdo. Even the microphone makes an appearance!

MACO CUSTODIO

SHOES TO SMILE FOR

Lamore says a shoe "is an object that already exists before even being worn . . . This 'object' quality has a certain mystery to it, akin to a sculpture with a life of its own." And her handmade shoes, small but stunning works of art, are evidence of that truth. A rose made of hand-dyed silk and leather cups the heel in "Sentiment Profond," while a jewel-studded agate and onyx bee with rock-crystal wings rests on the overlapping silk petals at the toe. The carved heel is made of 18-carat gold.

Lamore says she gets ideas from "almost everything," and clearly, nature is among her sources of inspiration. Her colorful "Bird of Paradise" peep-toe platform shoes are adorned with exotic feathers. At the back, "wings" sprout from the sides while ribbon-like feathers curl up from the top of the heel, recalling the tails of the shoe's namesake.

Gorgeous Lesage embroidery—found in the collections of couturiers from Elsa Schiaparelli to Yves Saint Laurent to Jean Paul Gautier—adorns Lamore's "Angel's Dew." A tiny gold bird clings to the back of the heel. Could it be one of the forty-one species of weaver bird found in the Central African Republic? The crystal-studded embroidery recalls the intricately woven nests of these small social birds.

Where there are birds, cats are sure to be lurking nearby. In "Leopardo," the ankle strap is formed by a leopard made of shaved mink with silk-screened spots, its tail draping gracefully down behind the 18-karat gold heel. Tiny onyx stones form the spots on the leopard's gold head and paws. A gold chain serves as a leash connecting the leopard to the toe loop, also fashioned of gold and lined with mink.

"Design is important,
but comfort is paramount."

—Manolo Blahnik

A collector of botanical drawings, Blahnik often draws from nature in his work. His spring/summer 2012 collection boasts footwear designed from what he calls his "botanical nonsense." The "Acantus" takes its name from the acanthus, a flowering plant that has bright green leaves similar to those of an oak tree—thus the acorns attached to the ends of the laces. The stacked spheres that make up the heel are the equivalent of silver beads, in this case, strung on a steel spine to support the foot.

The carnation is the national flower of Spain, Blahnik's birthplace. Although many think these voluptuous flowers are vulgar, he thinks they are fun—and also "make the perfect pompoms." That makes three good reasons to embellish his "Culona" design with three satin chiffon carnations. Blahnik would also know that the Spanish *culona* is slang for a woman with a voluptuous derriere. That is not an insult but a compliment. In fact, to say someone has a *culona* is the equivalent of saying she is very lucky!

Blahnik has said, "It is incredibly pretentious to say one is inspired by an artist, but there is no escaping it. I love Matisse." This admiration is evident in "Amiela," in which the designer drew from the artist's colorful, densely patterned work. The result is a decorative high heel that combines a sinuous strip of black leather with red trim and small black dots hand-painted on the white skin of a water snake.

By contrast, Blahnik's lime green satin mule, "Cartunates," is an exercise in elegant simplicity. The heel of stacked silver spheres and eyelets enhanced with tiny rhinestones would add just the right amount of shimmer and sparkle to catch the eye, as they peep out from beneath the skirt of a glamorous evening gown in matching silk satin or layers of airy chiffon.

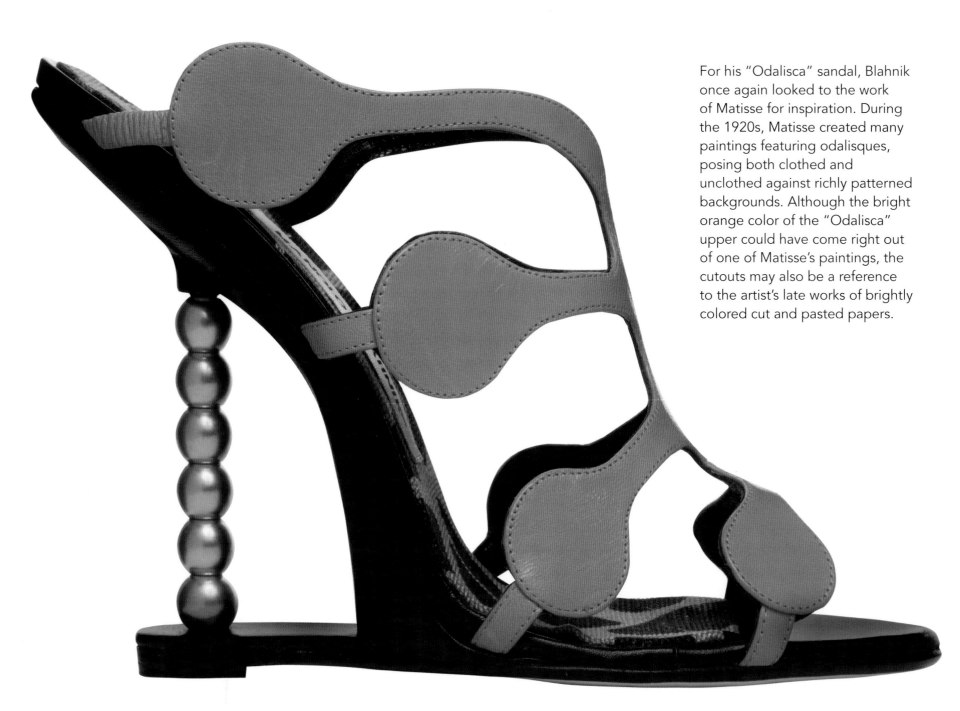

For his "Odalisca" sandal, Blahnik once again looked to the work of Matisse for inspiration. During the 1920s, Matisse created many paintings featuring odalisques, posing both clothed and unclothed against richly patterned backgrounds. Although the bright orange color of the "Odalisca" upper could have come right out of one of Matisse's paintings, the cutouts may also be a reference to the artist's late works of brightly colored cut and pasted papers.

In the late 1970s, Blahnik created his first heel-less shoe, the "Gruyere," a bright purple slingback with big orange dots. Over the years, he remained fascinated by the idea of no-heel shoes, and in 2006, he created two styles. One was called "Bhutan," and a model of it is now in The Metropolitan Museum of Art. The second style is called "Arunium," and was used by fashion designer Jean Paul Gaultier in his fall/winter 2006–07 haute couture show. Blahnik's sketch of "Arunium" (left) is just as delightful as the finished sandal.

MARLOES TEN BHÖMER
CHANGING CONVENTIONS

While studying 3D product design at the Higher School of Arts in Arnhem, the Netherlands, Marloes ten Bhömer was introduced to shoe design by one of her tutors, Marijke Bruggink, a founder of the footwear company Lola Pagola. The complexity involved in designing shoes drew Ten Bhömer in, and she focused on footwear design while getting her MA at the Royal College of Arts in London. Ten Bhömer is interested in "designing objects that ignore or criticize conventions in order to make the product world less generic." Although concept comes first for the designer, she realizes that "shoes need to be structurally sound."

It took two years for Ten Bhömer to develop "Beigefoldedshoe" from a concept into a wearable shoe. Each one is made from a single piece of vegetable-tanned leather folded around a stainless steel heel support, and each pair takes about a week and a half to make.

To construct the avant-garde "Carbonfibreshoe #1," Ten Bhömer used four pieces of carbon fiber. The unusual design, with the vertical heel on the outside of the foot, doesn't support normal weight distribution, so anyone courageous enough to wear a pair has to pay close attention to the way she sets one foot in front of another.

When Ten Bhömer was a child, she once re-created a pair of her mother's high heels in papier-mâché. To reproduce the same effect in her "Mâché" shoes, the designer invented a leather laminating technique that eliminates the need for a pattern to make the upper. It also allows for her to vary the thickness of the shoe, so that, no matter how unconventional the outside shape may be, the inside conforms exactly to the foot.

Ten Bhömer is constantly experimenting with nontraditional technologies and material techniques. Her "RotationalMouldedShoe" was designed specifically for the 2009 "After Hours" installation in the Krannert Art Museum at the University of Illinois. A negative mold based on the original design was generated by a computer. It was then placed in a rotation-molding machine and filled with liquid polyurethane rubber. As the mold rotated, the material solidified against the inner walls of the mold, creating a hollow form. The heel has a stainless steel support.

Instead of being molded or assembled, the "Rapidprototypedshoe" is printed out. Of course, this isn't as simple as it sounds. Employing Ten Bhömer's design and a model of a person's foot, a three-dimensional printer applies layers of polymer materials that are UV cured to construct a physical shoe. Ten Bhömer says that "the shoe is designed in such a way that it can be dismantled for the purpose of replacing parts."

Ten Bhömer's "Noheelsleathershoe" was an experiment in creating a heel-less shoe in the rotational molding technique used in the "Rotationalmouldedshoe (page 102)." The result is an unusual mule that makes it look as if the wearer is walking on tiptoe. A rectangular cutout in the upper of this otherwise blocky shoe reveals the shape of the foot.

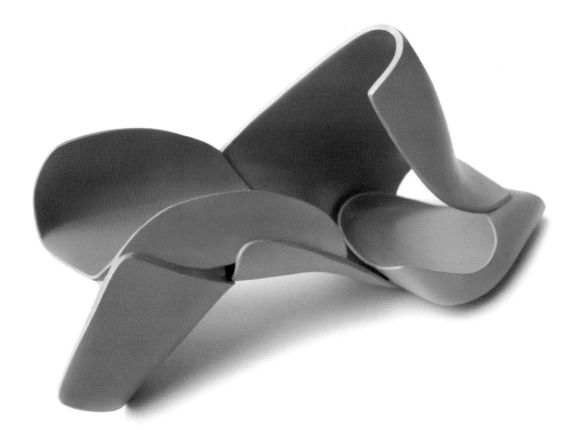

"Mouldedleathershoe2" (left) is all about the shapes used to build it. The vegetable-tanned leather pieces were shaped on various shoe lasts, then cut and assembled into a unique shoe.

To make her streamlined "Pressedleathershoe" (right), Ten Bhomer soaked three pieces of leather in water, then pressed them in a mold to form a three-dimensional shape. When the pieces were shaped and dried, she trimmed and assembled them around a last.

MASAYA KUSHINO

EXOTIC CHIMERAS

Masaya Kushino graduated with a major in fashion design from Kyoto University of Art and Design. Afterward, he traveled to Milan to get his masters at the Istituto Marangoni. On his return to Japan, he worked as a designer and stylist for artists and celebrities. In 2007, Kushino won the Japanese Leather and Leather Goods Industry Association (JILA) award and decided to start his own label, concentrating on exotic leather shoes and bags.

Based in Kyoto, Kushino works with local artisans to realize his animal-inspired creations, which he calls "chimeras" because they are hybrids fabricated from feathers, leather, horsehair—even antlers and faux rams' horns. Long sprays of peacock tail feathers burst from the intricately carved heel of his iridescent shoe named, appropriately enough, the "Peacock" (opposite page).

Kushino collaborated with
the Japanese fashion house
Somarta on their fall/winter
2010–11 runway show, creating
boots and shoes with furry
ponytails that gave a flirty little
flip with every step the models
took. The high heels combined
flora and fauna, with a lion's
paw at the base morphing into
a snake that, in turn, morphed
into a spray of decorative
leaves cupping the heel.

The heel-less shoes Kushino calls "Lung-ta" (Tibetan for "horse of wind"; above left) also have tails, but these are made of hair. The metallic gold lace on the uppers, the light wood of the soles, and the pale blond hair are intended the express the glare of bright light. In contrast, his black "lung-tshup-ta" ("horse of storm") boots (above right) boots feature permed hair and leather uppers tooled with a pattern that could represent lightning.

From the front. Kushino's "Aries" shoes (left) could almost be mistaken for oxfords embellished with white fur. But these oxfords have a twist—literally. The leather high heel of each shoe is shaped and stitched to resemble a ram's horn. In astrology, Aries, the ram, is the first sign in the zodiac. The sign is associated with leadership, energy and drive— clearly, characteristics Kushino demonstrates in his designs.

Glittery black antlers sprout from the sides of the high platform soles of "Ceryneian-Hind" (opposite page), ensuring that no one will follow the wearer too closely. The name of the shoe comes from Greek mythology. The Hind of Cerynaea, also known as the Golden Hind for its gold antlers, was a deer sacred to Artemis, the goddess of the hunt.

With two pairs of booties from the Structures & Megastructures collection, Albu turns perceptions upside down. In one pair (opposite page), adding a heel to the toes makes you question which way is up. With the other (right), you may need to look twice (or thrice) before you realize that what you're seeing is not a reflection, but an upended version of the top half of the shoe being used as a support. Can you walk in them? The answer is yes—at least if you're a runway model.

115

In another shoe from his Structures & Megastructures collection, Mihai Albu traded witty plays on perception for a normal high-heel shoe. Or has he? Are those metal cones sprouting from the vamp and heel the tops of rockets taking off in different directions? Or could they be stylized versions of medieval towers, such as the Tower of Stefan the Great in the foothills of Romania's Carpathian Mountains?

Albu has mentioned Antoni Gaudí as a major source of inspiration in his work, and the Spanish architect's influence can easily be seen in this shoe from Albu's Aequilibrium collection. The feeling of a structure within a structure, the shape of the arch, and even the colors and textures are reminiscent of the roof of a building (above) at the entrance to Gaudí's Park Güell in Barcelona. The small metal balls, one at each end of the shoe add a touch of Gaudí-style fantasy.

With these shoes (left and opposite page), Albu seems to have turned to Cubist sculpture for his inspiration. First seen in the work of Pablo Picasso and Georges Braque, Cubist artists deconstructed the object before reassembling it in an abstract form. Like all sculpture, Albu's shoes have to be viewed from different angles to get the full effect. In fact, some buyers may be more comfortable putting these shoes on a pedestal than on their feet.

119

Here, fantasy seems to be the rule.
A sandal (opposite page, left) has
three heels, one of which forms a
cornucopia curving across the instep,
beads spilling like fruit from its open
end. A red-winged butterfly turned
on its side becomes the heel of a
metallic blue platform shoe (opposite
page, right). Yet, if it weren't for the
antennae, the butterfly could be seen
as a mask for a masquerade party.
In another shoe (right), peacock
feathers swoop up from the back to
cup the heel and the calf of the leg.
But from the back, you can see that a
skull forms the shape the feathers are
attached to, giving them the aspect
of a ritual headdress.

121

NAÄM BEN

Play with Me

Naäm Ben is the label created by designer Amar Nasri. A few years after graduating from the AFPIC School of Shoe Design in Paris, he started his own company and launched his first collection, called Amalgam. After designing several footwear collections for men, he began designing shoes for women as well.

Nasri's collection Come and Play with Me was inspired by the work of Greg Lynn, an architect and sculptor whose colorful furniture made from recycled toys won the Golden Lion Award for the Best Installation project in the International Exhibition at the Venice Architecture Biennale. Working on a smaller scale, Nasri affixes miniature toys found in flea markets and garage sales to create whimsical confections that are as charming as they are playful.

In "Toys on Sole" (opposite page), delicate uppers consisting only of narrow black laces offer a surprising contrast to platform soles covered with a multitude of colorful tiny plastic figurines. In the "Softtoys" boot (left), finger puppets and other small plush animals crowd together as though to cuddle the foot on a cold blustery day.

RENÉ VAN DEN BERG
From Orthopedics to High Fashion

René van den Berg's family has been involved one way or another in the business of making shoes since 1902. When it came time to go to university, Van den Berg chose a stable profession and became a technical specialist in orthopedic shoes. After ten years, however, his love of art and fashion won out, and he opened his own studio to create custom-made shoes in 1992.

"Hommage à Giger" (opposite page) was among Van den Berg's early designs. Despite being made from natural materials (wood, calf leather, and suede), the shoe looks futuristic—almost like something menacing you'd expect to see in a scary science fiction movie. Not surprising, given that it was designed as a tribute to H. R. Giger, the Swiss surrealist artist and set designer who won an Oscar for Best Visual Effects for his work on the 1979 film *Alien*, which included his design for the title creature.

The heel of "Hapexa," another early design, looks like part of a spinal column with the ribs wrapping around to protect the red heart of the shoe. But does the design on the front represent a shield for added protection from the outside world or a cage intended to protect the outside world from the wild heart trapped inside? While van den Berg was designing the shoe, he was reading British author Clive Barker's novel *Imajica*, about five worlds ruled by the tyrannical god Hapexamendios, the Unbeheld. As soon as Van den Berg, who has synesthesia and sees each letter and number in a particular color, saw the word *Hapexamendios*, he realized that the colors of the first six letters matched the colors of his shoe and—*voila!*—the shoe had its name.

Black suede and sting-ray leather form the upper of "Terminus Est." The ray leather and shape of the graceful sculptural heel bring to mind the sea, with a breaker starting at the ankle and surging over the heel of the foot before ending in gentle ripples at the sole. But considering the name, one might also infer a darker reference, and see the heel as the hilt and the pointed toe as the tip of the executioner's sword wielded by Severian in Gene Wolfe's science fiction series The Book of the New Sun. But not so. Van den Berg was commissioned to make a pair shoes for a client's wife and, for the first time, was given free rein to design the shoes however he liked. He says he named the design "Terminus Est" in the sense of a dividing line because "Creating these shoes was like crossing a border to me."

Van den Berg gained recognition for his designs when he won the Henk Overduin prize in 1996. But his new career really took off when fashion designer Thierry Mugler saw the shoes van den Berg had designed for the diploma collection of a young friend, leading to the creation of footwear for five of Mugler's runway collections. Since then, Van den Berg has collaborated with several fashion designers, including Ilja Visser, founder of the couture label ILJA.

"Ambacht" was inspired by the architectural elements and colors of Pierre Cuyper's Rijksmuseum in Amsterdam, where Visser presented her spring/ summer 2011 collection. The graphic design and stability of the shoes are in deliberate contrast to the more organic shapes of the clothing.

Visser's fall/winter 2011–12 collection was inspired by Hyperborea—in Greek mythology, a mythical country "beyond the north wind" where the sun never sets—mountain climbing, and the elegance of modern couture. The black straps of the stylishly high sandals recall the rappelling gear used to scale the steep slopes of a snow-covered mountain, while the open white sole could easily be mistaken for a perilous crevasse to be navigated by the climber.

Klavers van Engelen, winner of the 2007 Mercedes-Benz Dutch Fashion Award, is the avant-garde fashion label founded by Dutch designers Neils Klavers and Astrid van Engelen. The collaboration of Klavers, Van Engelen, and Van den Berg produced a pump with a chunky block heel in stark contrast to the otherwise feminine shape of the shoe as well as to the soft fabric and flowing lines of the clothing in the label's spring/summer 2012 collection.

Cadabra says she designed her turquoise "Water Lily" sandal "to symbolize a carefree summer." The epitome of femininity, the sandal features colorful three-dimensional flowers perched at the end of iridescent lavender and pale blue "stems" that wind delicately around the foot, capturing "the essence of a lazy summer day." This shoe is a beautiful update of her original pink and black shoe of the same name.

The "Rocket" shoe features a flaming rocket crashing into the front in a burst of stars. Appropriately enough, Cadabra was inspired to design the shoe when she was invited to a friend's fireworks party. Made of suede, the shoe incorporates a plastic prismatic fabric called Shimmertex in its shining tail flame and star-spangled explosion.

United Nude's "Eamz" shoe pays tribute to Charles and Ray Eames, the American husband and wife design team best known for their chair designs. Mimicking the foot of an office chair in the Eames' Aluminum Group, the reflective cast-aluminum "Eamz" heel practically disappears into the environment, making the back of the foot look as if it's suspended in midair. Like most United Nude shoes, "Eamz" comes in a variety of styles, including the "Eamz X Elastic" sandal, which is held to the foot with two wide elastic bands.

The "Crazy Lacy" may have been inspired by hiking boots, but the only trail this colorful boot belongs on is the high road to fashion. Luckily, all those laces are just for show. Tucked on the inner side of the boot is a simple side zipper that bypasses the need to fuss with tying and untying laces.

Although the name, "Web Hi," might bring a spiderweb to mind, the design of the laser-cut leather upper and matching metal heel of this peep-toe bootie looks more like a Voronoi diagram. Named after its creator, Ukrainian mathematician Georgy Vornoi, the diagram is often used in contemporary architecture to create organic-looking structures. With "Web Hi," United Nude has turned it into high fashion.

"90 Degree" appears to be balanced precariously on a high, thin heel that forms a perfect right angle at floor level. But despite its fragile look, the heel is made of the same tough carbon fiber used to manufacture parts for racecars and yachts. Add its double platform, one of wood and one of rubber, and the "90 Degree" sandal reaches a height of 6.7 inches.

The Japanese-inspired "Geisha" combines elements of the okobo platform sandal, worn by apprentice geishas, and the obi, the decorative cloth that wraps around the waist of the traditional kimono. In United Nude's shoe, the boldly colored elastic "obi" wraps around the molded platform to hold the shoe snugly in place. The "obi," in turn, is held in place by a wide strip of leather that runs up from the sole to form a strap around the back of the ankle. Another narrower strap starts at the sole and crosses over the toes at an angle, completing the surprisingly elegant structure.

Clearly architectural in concept, United Nude's edgy "Frame Rivet" uses a leather-covered, openwork carbon fiber structure to connect the heel to the upper. The elasticated leather straps that frame the foot are fastened together with rivets. The angles created by the seamless construction of the sandal recall those seen in a truss bridge.

The collaboration between United Nude and fashion designer Iris van Herpen began in 2010 and has resulted in an array of extraordinary styles. The designs begin with sketches from Van Herpen, then United Nude figures out whether it's possible to make the shoes, and the two work together to develop them. Koolhaas has said that "Creating new shoes with Iris is a greater challenge each time," but seeing the shoes on the runway is one of the "artistic highlights of the year."

The ultra-conceptual "Capriole" takes its name from Van Herpen's fall/winter 2011–12 collection. The high, curving heels were designed with the aid of a computer and printed with 3D rapid prototyping before being reinforced with laminated carbon fiber. The uppers were made from a material developed by Bart Hess.

Created for MICRO, Van Herpen's spring/summer 2012 collection, "Fang" (below) takes its name from the ten recurved fang-like structures that support the foot. Made of fiberglass and carbon fiber, the soles are created in a slow molding process.

Their most recent collaboration, a bootie called "Thorn" (right) was created for Hybrid Holism, Van Herpen's fall/winter 2012–13 collection. From the front, the smooth, slow-molded shoes look rather plain, but the side view is a another matter. An arch of eight wicked-looking spikes made of sharp, hand-cut semiprecious stones pierce the uppers between platform and heel, creating an entirely different look.

VICTORIA SPRUCE

Shoes with a Twist

For as long as she can remember, Victoria Spruce has wanted to design shoes. After she received her BA (with honors) from Cordwainers College in London, she got her MA in women's footwear design from the Royal College of Art. Spruce describes her design style as "modern, clean, and forward thinking." She enjoys experimenting with materials and technology, and her "strong belief in the fluidity of line" leads her to emphasize shape and silhouette in her designs.

In 2010, Spruce was one of three finalists for the Drapers' Student Footwear Designer of the Year Award, and the following year she won a Footwear Friends Annual Award. In April 2012, Spruce was named one of ten finalists in the accessories category of the ITS (International Talent Support) competition, giving her the opportunity to show her work in Trieste, Italy, in July.

Organic structural forms and architectural structure are among Victoria Spruce's inspirations, and she says that she loves "taking elements of something much bigger and scaling them down to a wearable shoe." Her spring 2012 collection provides a dramatic contrast between modern technology and traditional shoemaking in its combination of 3D printing and hard, shiny synthetics with soft leathers. Spruce feels that the upper and heel of a shoe should be conceived as a whole rather than as two separate pieces, and the graceful flowing lines of her shoes are a testimony to that belief.